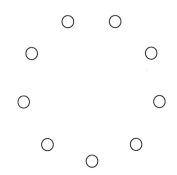

The Fasting Practice

Practicing the Way

Welcome

Welcome to the Fasting Practice. For over a thousand years, fasting was one of the central practices of the Way of Jesus. It was common practice for apprentices of Jesus to fast twice a week until sundown — on Wednesdays and Fridays, as well as the 40 days of Lent. Similar to essential spiritual disciplines like prayer or the reading of Scripture or church on Sunday, fasting was simply one of the things that practicing Christians did.

After all, Jesus began his life's work with 40 days of fasting, a practice he continued throughout his lifetime. And he said, "Follow me." It makes sense that we would follow his example and incorporate fasting — in both longer and shorter intervals — into our Rule of Life, or our overall life architecture of discipleship to Jesus.

And yet, very few followers of Jesus in the modern West fast at all.

There are all sorts of reasons for this: the influence of the Enlightenment, cultural hedonism, the widespread availability of food because of modern agribusiness, the (false) advertising of the food industry telling us that we need three meals a day, the confusion of appetite with hunger (which are not the same thing), or the struggle with disordered eating and body shame, etc. But the greatest reason is likely the West's emphasis on the mind over the body. This focus on rational thought has given us all sorts of breakthroughs in science, medicine, and technology, but it has left us disembodied; we've lost sight of the human as a whole person — mind and body and soul.

Fasting is one of the most essential and powerful of all the practices of Jesus and one of the best ways we have to integrate our entire person, including our body, around God.

Over the next four weeks, we will cover the four reasons we fast.

01 To offer ourselves to Jesus
02 To grow in holiness
03 To amplify our prayers
04 To stand with the poor

But remember: The ultimate aim of fasting is to get in touch with our hunger for God. Hunger is the state of wanting or needing something you do not have. When we fast, we awaken our body and soul to its deep yearning for life with the Father. We become able to say with Jesus, "I have food to eat that you know nothing about." (John 4v32)

"Fasting gives birth to prophets, she strengthens the powerful; fasting makes lawgivers wise. She is a safeguard for the soul, a steadfast companion for the body, a weapon for the brave, and a discipline for champions. Fasting repels temptations, anoints for godliness. She is a companion for sobriety, the crafter of a sound mind. In wars she fights bravely, in peace she teaches tranquility."

—ST. BASIL THE GREAT (A.D. 330-379)

Table of Contents

Tips

This Companion Guide is full of spiritual exercises, best practices, and good advice on the spiritual discipline of fasting.

But it's important to note that the Practices are not formulaic. We can't use them to control our spiritual formation, or even our relationship with God. Sometimes they don't even work very well. Sometimes we fast and we experience spiritual breakthroughs and miracles, but other times we just feel tired and hangry. That's okay. Our goal isn't to control our spiritual formation, but to *surrender* to Jesus. To give more and more of our deepest selves to him to rescue and save and heal and transform, in his time, his way, by his power and peace and presence.

The key with the spiritual disciplines is to let go of outcomes and just offer them up to Jesus in love.

Because it's so easy to lose sight of the ultimate aim of a Practice, here are a few tips to keep in mind as you fast.

01   Start small

Start where you are, not where you "should" be. If a full day of fasting a week is too much, start with one meal and break the fast at lunch instead of dinner. The smaller the start, the better chance you have of really sticking to it and growing over time.

02   Think subtraction, not addition

Please do not add fasting into your already overbusy, overfull life. You are likely already stressed and tired. Instead, on your fasting day(s), think: What can I cut out? How can I slow my day down? Where can I find a little more time to pray and focus on God? Formation is about less, not more. About slowing down and simplifying your life around what matters most: life with Jesus.

03   You get out what you put in

The more fully you give yourself to this Practice, the more life-changing it will be; the more you just dabble with it, the more shortcuts you take, the less of an effect it will have on your transformation.

04   Remember the J-curve

Experts on learning tell us that whenever we set out to master a new skill, it tends to follow a J-shaped curve; we tend to get worse before we get better. You may not even notice if you go half a day without eating due to busyness with work or school or life, but when you try fasting, you might wake up with your stomach screaming at you! That's okay. Expect it to be hard at first; it will get easier in time. Just stay with the Practice.

05   There is no formation without repetition

Spiritual formation is slow, deep, cumulative work that takes years, not weeks. The goal of this four-week experience is just to get you *started* on a journey of a lifetime. Upon completion of this Practice, you will have a map for the journey ahead and hopefully some possible companions for the Way. But what you do next is up to you.

A note about the Reach Exercise

We recognize that we're all at different places in our stage of discipleship and season of life. To that end, we've added a Reach Exercise to each of the four weeks for those of you who have the time, energy, and desire to go further in fasting.

Additionally, we have weekly reading and corresponding episodes from the Rule of Life podcast to enhance all four sessions. Enjoy!

A note about the recommended reading

Fasting is an ancient practice, but it's still a new discipline for most of us in the West. Reading a book alongside the Practice can greatly help your understanding and enjoyment of this discipline. You may love to read, or you may not. For that reason, it's recommended, but certainly not required.

Our companion book for the Fasting Practice is *God's Chosen Fast* by Arthur Wallis. It's an older book, so be gracious with the antiquated examples and language, but it's full of wisdom, insight, and scriptural truth, as well as practical advice.

May God himself,
the God of peace,
sanctify you through
and through. May
your whole spirit, soul
and body be kept
blameless at the
coming of our Lord
Jesus Christ.

—1 Thessalonians 5v23

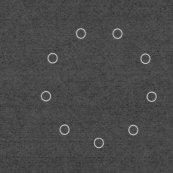

To Offer Ourselves to Jesus

WEEK 01

Overview

In the modern world, you are more likely to hear about fasting from a Muslim, Buddhist, nutrition expert, or fitness guru than from a serious disciple of Jesus. Most followers of Jesus in the West no longer fast; if they do, it's rarely on a weekly basis, despite the fact that it was the common practice of the church for well over a millennium and a half to do so.

Yet in his teaching on fasting in Matthew 6v16, Jesus said, "*When* you fast," not "*If* you fast". He assumed his apprentices would follow his example and incorporate fasting into their discipleship.

What if we are missing out on one of the most essential and powerful of all the practices of Jesus?

One of the reasons fasting has fallen by the wayside in the Western church is we have lost sight of what Pope John Paul II called a "theology of the body." This is the biblical theology of the human as a whole person. In the biblical view, you don't *have* a body, you *are* a body; your body is a part of who you are.

As powerful as the mind is, because we are holistic beings, we can't simply think our way into spiritual maturity. Our discipleship to Jesus must take seriously our body, as it is "the temple of the Holy Spirit" — a home where we make room for God to dwell.

Most of us are used to approaching our spiritual formation and life with God through the door of our mind — by thinking, talking, praying, reading, or hearing teaching and preaching. But very few of us are comfortable approaching our spiritual formation through our stomach, or our body as a whole.

Fasting is one of the best disciplines we have to reintegrate our mind to our body, and offer our whole selves to God in surrender.

Practice

WEEK 01: TO OFFER OURSELVES TO JESUS

For the Fasting Practice, each week's exercise will be very similar and straightforward: fast the most common way, one full day until sundown. Each week, we will attempt to focus our heart on the reason for fasting we covered in that week's session.

01 **Fast until sundown one day this week, focusing on offering yourself to Jesus**

- Pick a day that works for you. Wednesdays or Fridays are ideal if you want to get in touch with Christians around the world and throughout church history.

- If possible, pick a day to do this together as a community; this will help to encourage and enliven your weekly practice.

- Fast until sundown that day. Then, eat a simple meal in gratitude.

- If a full day is too much for your body or soul, start smaller. Skip breakfast and break the fast at lunch or 3 p.m. Remember: The

goal is to make fasting a part of your regular life, not try it once or twice, hate it, and never try it again. Start where you are, not where you feel like you "should" be.

- In the time you'd normally be grocery shopping, cooking, eating, or cleaning, give yourself to prayer. Let your desire for food point you to Jesus as you open yourself to him.

- In your dedicated times of prayer, or each time a hunger pain comes, you may want to pray Romans 12v1-2, or simply, "God, I offer my body to you in worship. Please transform me."

- As you go about your day — your morning commute, caregiving, email, errands — just enjoy God's company and attempt to open your heart to him all through the day.

A few basic tips

01   Drink tons of water to stay hydrated (unless you choose to do a total fast, no food *or* water).

02   If you normally drink coffee to wake up, you may want to still have coffee to avoid a caffeine headache, but just have it black. Coffee is 99.9% water and will not keep your body from entering the fasting state.

03   The more time you can give to prayer and reflection, and the less busy you are that day, the better. Make it your goal to slow down the day you fast, and be present to your body, and God, as much as you possibly can. You may want to find a park on your lunch break or take a few short walks throughout your day. Give as much attention to God as is doable.

04   Resist the urge to judge your experience. Release thoughts like, "I liked it; I disliked it." "I felt close to God; I didn't feel close to God." Just let the experience of fasting be what it is, and offer it to God in love.

NOTES

Reach Practice

Reading

Read chapters 1-5 of *God's Chosen Fast* by Arthur Wallis.

Podcast

Listen to episode 1 of the Fasting series from the Rule of Life podcast by Practicing the Way.

Exercise: Fast for two days

This week's Reach Exercise is to fast for two days, like the early Christians. You may want to adopt the Wednesday and Friday rhythm like they did, or pick different days that work better for your schedule. But avoid fasting on the Sabbath or the Lord's Day, as Sunday is for feasting, not fasting.

NOTES

Fasting Reflection

Reflection is a key component in our spiritual formation.

Millenia ago, King David prayed in Psalm 139v23-24:

> Search me, God, and know my heart;
>   test me and know my anxious thoughts.
> See if there is any offensive way in me,
>   and lead me in the way everlasting.

Trevor Hudson, a scholar on Ignatian spirituality, has said, "We don't change from our experience, we change when we reflect on our experience."

If you want to get the most out of this Practice, you need to do it, and then *reflect* on it.

Before your next time together with the group for Week 2, take five to ten minutes to journal out your answers to the following three questions.

01   What was your experience like?

02   Where did you feel resistance?

03   Where did you feel delight?

Note: As you write, be as specific as possible. While bullet points are just fine, if you write it out in narrative form, your brain will be able to process your insights in a more lasting way.

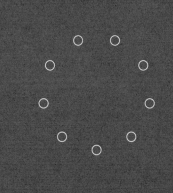

To Grow in Holiness

WEEK 02

Overview

St. Augustine of Hippo, when asked, "Why fast?" said, "Because it is sometimes necessary to check the delight of the flesh in respect to licit pleasures in order to keep it from yielding to illicit joys."

Like most ancient Christian intellectuals, he saw gluttony as the first of the seven deadly sins, and saw a Christian's relationship to food as a key part of their relationship to God. Most of us can see this link by direct experience: An inability to control one's appetite has a ripple effect across the whole person, often resulting in a corresponding inability to control other bodily appetites — for drink, sex, speech, gossip, consumerism, power, and dominion over others.

But on the flip side, many luminaries from the Way of Jesus have considered fasting to be a way to feed your spirit and starve your flesh, the part of our person that is bent toward sin.

When we fast, at least four things are happening in our body and soul.

01   It's weaning us off the pleasure principle

02   It's revealing what's in our heart

03   It's re-ordering our desires

04   It's drawing on the power of God to overcome sin

Our fight is not *against* the body — the body is broken, but it is a good gift.
Our fight is *for* the body. It's against the flesh, or sinful appetites within us
all. And fasting is one of the most powerful disciplines of the Way to free our
body and soul from the chains of sin and the prison of shame.

Practice

WEEK 02: TO GROW IN HOLINESS

01   Fast until sundown one day this week, focusing on growing in holiness

- Pick a day that works for you. Again, Wednesdays or Fridays are ideal if you want to get in touch with Christians around the world and throughout church history.

- If possible, pick a day to do this together as a community; this will help to encourage and enliven your weekly practice.

- Fast until sundown that day. Then, eat a simple meal in gratitude.

- If a full day is too much for your body or soul, start smaller. Skip breakfast and break the fast at lunch or 3 p.m. Each week, try to stretch your fast time a little longer. If last week was until noon, try for 2 p.m. this week.

- In the time you'd normally be grocery shopping, cooking, eating, or cleaning, give yourself to prayer, and focus your heart on this second motivation for fasting: to grow in holiness.

- In your dedicated times of prayer, or each time a hunger pain comes, you may want to pray, "God, purify my heart and purge my whole person of sin."

- If possible, set aside time in the quiet or in deep conversation with a close spiritual friend, and ask God to reveal any sin in your life he is targeting for freedom. Offer it to God in confession, repentance, and prayer.

NOTES

Reach Practice

WEEK 02: TO GROW IN HOLINESS

Reading

Read chapters 6-10 of *God's Chosen Fast* by Arthur Wallis.

Podcast

Listen to episode 2 of the Fasting series from the Rule of Life podcast by Practicing the Way.

Exercise: Fast for two days

This week's Reach Exercise is the same as last week: to fast for a second day, like the early Christians.

You may want to adopt the Wednesday and Friday rhythm like they did, or pick different days that work better for your schedule. But avoid fasting on the Sabbath or the Lord's Day, as Sunday is for feasting, not fasting.

NOTES

Fasting Reflection

WEEK 02: TO GROW IN HOLINESS

Before your next time together with the group for Week 3, take five to ten minutes to journal out your answers to the following three questions.

---

01 Did you notice any shift in your heart toward sin while you were fasting?

---

02 What's an area in your life where your willpower is failing and you are praying for the grace to change?

---

03 What's an area in your life where you are experiencing increasing freedom from sin and joy in God?

Note: As you write, be as specific as possible. While bullet points are just fine, if you write it out in narrative form, your brain will be able to process your insights in a more lasting way.

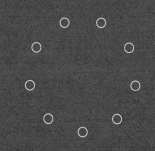

To Amplify Our Prayers

WEEK 03

Overview

Fasting and prayer go together. Like two wings of a bird, together they take flight. You can pray without fasting, and you can fast without praying, but when you combine the two, there's a noticeable amplification of our prayer before God. This comes as no surprise, since fasting is a kind of praying with our body. When the request of our heart is coupled with the yearning of our body, our prayer is purified of its dross and presented like a precious metal before the Father, for him to do as he will.

Of course, "prayer" is an umbrella term for the medium through which we communicate and commune with God. Prayer involves both speaking and listening. And fasting is a key companion in both.

Fasting is an aid in *hearing God*.

It helps us to discern his voice through the noise and distraction of our lives.
It sharpens our mind; in the fasting state, our mind is more alert, focused, and
open. It makes it easier for us to hear how God is coming to us and to hear
his will and direction for our lives.

But fasting is also an aid to *being heard by God.*

It helps us to break through the walls that stand between us and the release
of God's plans, purposes, and power. Story after story — in Scripture and
church history — attest to this reality: When prayer and fasting link arms, it's
often the tipping point in the struggle to release God's Kingdom, on earth as
it is in heaven.

Practice

01   **Fast for one day, focusing on how it amplifies your prayers**

- Pick a day that works for you; we recommend Wednesdays or Fridays.

- If possible, pick a day that works for your community to fast together.

- Fast until sundown that day. Then, eat a simple meal in gratitude.

- In the time you'd normally be grocery shopping, cooking, eating, or cleaning, give yourself to prayer.

- In your dedicated times of prayer, or each time a hunger pain comes, you may want to pray through a short list of specific requests you are holding before God, or simply pray, "God, speak to me, I'm listening."

- If possible, set aside time in the quiet to listen for God's voice and offer your prayers up to God. You may want to get up early, find a quiet park on your lunch break, or end your day with a nice walk. But find a time and place to minimize distractions, and combine your fasting to prayer.

NOTES

Reach Practice

WEEK 03: TO AMPLIFY OUR PRAYERS

Reading

Read chapters 11-15 of *God's Chosen Fast* by Arthur Wallis.

Podcast

Listen to episode 3 of the Fasting series from the Rule of Life podcast by Practicing the Way.

Exercise: Fast for a longer period of time

If you have the desire and life space to increase the duration of your fasting practice, this could be an ideal week to do a longer fast.

You may want to fast for a full day, eating dinner one night and not breaking the fast until the morning 36 hours later.

Or you may feel invited by the Spirit of Jesus into a multi-day fast of two days, three days, or longer.

Just remember: Unless there is a *clear* stirring in your heart from the Spirit to pursue a longer fast, the best practice is to "walk before you run." If you've only ever fasted until sundown, try just going until the following morning as your next step in the journey.

NOTES

Fasting Reflection

WEEK 03: LISTENING TO GOD

Before your next time together with the group for Week 4, take five to ten minutes to journal out your answers to the following three questions.

01   Did you sense God's voice this last week in any way?

02   What's one thing you were specifically praying for?

03   How are you feeling three weeks into this new Practice?

Note: As you write, be as specific as possible. While bullet points are just fine, if you write it out in narrative form, your brain will be able to process your insights in a more lasting way.

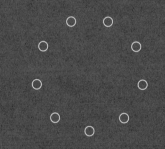

To Stand With the Poor

WEEK 04

Overview

"Give to the hungry what you deny your own appetite."
—St. Gregory of Nyssa

In the West, many of us struggle with the problem of food abundance —
having too much food to eat. Our pantries overflow with snacks; we have
so much food in our fridges it goes bad before we have a chance to eat it;
apps like DoorDash put any food we want just a few swipes away. Dieting
is a constant fad, and most of us live in a daily war of attrition against sugar,
processed carbs, and over-indulgence. But most of the world, and many
more people than we realize in our own neighborhoods and cities, live with
food scarcity — not having enough to eat. Often, they are hiding in plain
sight in our own churches and communities.

Fasting is a way to bridge this gap, between "the haves" and "the have
nots." Going back at least as far as Isaiah 58, it has long been a vehicle

for biblical justice, a way for those with too much food to share with those in need of food.

Early on in the history of the church, fasting was tied to what Jesus and the early Christians called "almsgiving" — a practice that combined generosity, serving, and justice. On fasting days, Christians would take the food or the money they would have spent on food and give it to the poor. Often, they would also give the time they would have spent cooking, eating, and cleaning up to serve the poor.

This simple practice of giving away the money we would have spent on ourselves has the potential to transform not only the lives of the poor, but our own lives and communities as well.

Practice

WEEK 04: TO STAND WITH THE POOR

01   Fast for one day, focusing on standing with the poor

Our exercise for Week 4 is very similar to the previous three weeks, with one simple addition: generosity and service to the poor.

- Pick a day that works for you; we recommend Wednesdays or Fridays.

- If possible, pick a day that works for your community to fast together.

- Fast until sundown that day, then eat a simple meal in gratitude.

- In the time you'd normally be grocery shopping, cooking, eating, or cleaning, give yourself to prayer.

- Calculate the money you would have spent on breakfast and lunch, and share it with the poor.

- Here are a few ideas of how to do this:

  - Donate the money or food to your local food bank or your church's food pantry.

  - Donate the funds to a local nonprofit.

  - Buy groceries for someone.

  - Share your money with someone who needs help paying a medical bill or unexpected expense.

  - Find a need and meet it that day.

  - Pray and ask God to infuse your imagination and desire with his imagination and desire. Do whatever comes to the surface of your heart.

- As you fast, give, and serve, quietly ask God to set your heart free of self-love and self-preservation and transform you into a person of Christlike agape.

Reach Practice

WEEK 04: TO STAND WITH THE POOR

Reading

Read chapters 16-20 of *God's Chosen Fast* by Arthur Wallis.

Podcast

Listen to episode 4 of the Fasting series from the Rule of Life podcast by Practicing the Way.

Exercise: Serve the poor

Our final Reach Exercise is to not only share your food money with the poor, but to also find a place to serve those in need in your city or community. To make a relational move toward the poor, treating them not as objects of pity, but as brothers and sisters.

You may want to serve with a local nonprofit or volunteer for a justice initiative with your church, or simply find someone you know with a practical need. The more relational the better.

The end goal isn't just to share with the poor, or even serve the poor, but become *family* with the poor. As you do, you will see the face of Jesus in often unexpected places.

NOTES

Fasting Reflection

WEEK 04: TO STAND WITH THE POOR

As you come to the end of this Practice, take five to ten minutes to journal out your answers to the following three questions.

01 After a month, what effect do you see this Practice having on your body and soul?

02 Are you thinking of continuing this Practice? If so, in what way?

03 How could you continue almsgiving in your city or community?

Note: As you write, be as specific as possible. While bullet points are just fine, if you write it out in narrative form, your brain will be able to process your insights in a more lasting way.

NOTES

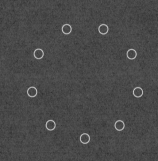

Keep Going

Continue the Journey

You are not going to explore the full scope of the ancient practice of fasting in four weeks. This short Practice is only designed to get you moving on a lifelong journey. The weekly fasting rhythm you've been practicing is meant to be integrated into your Rule of Life, should you so choose. You may choose to make fasting a *rhythmic* part of your discipleship, on a weekly or monthly basis, or you may want to practice *responsive* fasting, regularly responding to life's sacred events with all you've learned through this Practice.

Where you go from here is entirely up to you, but if you decide to integrate fasting into your life, here's a list of next steps to continue your practice.

Recommend Reading

01 *Fasting* by Scot McKnight

02 *The Spirituality of Fasting* by Charles M. Murphy

03 *Tony Evans Speaks Out On Fasting* by Tony Evans

Recommended Exercises

01 Go on a solitude retreat

Jesus went into the wilderness in silence, solitude, fasting, and Scripture. His "retreat" was 40 days long; yours can be much shorter. Start with an overnight. But you can emulate Jesus' foray into the wilderness by practicing fasting while in solitude and silence, and by immersing yourself in Scripture.

This would be an especially good idea if you're in a season of discernment and facing a major decision where you really desire to hear God's voice of direction.

02 Fast for a longer period of time

There's no "right" length, as fasting is never once commanded by Jesus or required by the New Testament writers. But many have found that a one-time or infrequent longer fast (of a week or 21 days) can be a before/after moment in one's spiritual journey.

The key is to only do this if you sense the Spirit's invitation. Do not practice this out of idealism, spiritual heroism, or a misplaced desire for weight loss or a spiritual high.

03 Call your church or community to a fast

You can organize a fast for a larger group of people around a specific aim, such as revival in your church or city.

It's best to meet daily during community-wide fasts, for prayer and mutual encouragement.

Made in United States
Troutdale, OR
11/04/2024